VIKING BOY
THE REAL STORY

TONY BRADMAN

**WALKER
BOOKS**

Þá mælti Gísli: "Það vissi eg fyrir löngu að eg var vel kvæntur en þó vissi eg eigi að eg væri svo vel kvæntur sem eg er."

Then Gísli said: "I have long known that I married well, but never till now just how well..."

(From *The Saga of Gísli Sursson*)

Deyr fé
deyja frændr
deyr sjálfr it sama
ek veit einn
at aldri deyr
dómr um dauðan hvern

Cattle die
kinsmen die too
death will also
come for you
but I know a thing
that never dies
the fame you gain
in others' eyes

(From The Hávamál, or The Words of the High One)

CONTENTS

Hail, stranger! My name is Gunnar,

and you might have read about my adventures in

the book Viking Boy. *In that tale – or saga as we*

call such things here in the North – I swore an oath

to avenge my father's murder, and I went on a long,

hard journey through the world

of the Vikings so I could fulfil it.

Now I have returned to take you on a journey of

your own through the same world. In this book

you will find out where and how we Vikings lived,

what beliefs we held and what we did, and you will

travel to the new lands we settled. You will meet my family and friends and many other Viking people, and even the great god Odin.

So find your warmest cloak, pull on a pair of strong boots, and make sure your sword is loose in the scabbard. There will be danger ahead, and the storm of blades in battle. But there will also be companions in longship and shield-wall, poetry by the hearth-fire, tough Viking men and women, and gleaming Viking treasure.

Are you ready? Then come with me...

ONE

HARD LANDS TO LIVE IN

YOUR JOURNEY begins with some Viking magic.

Imagine you are a shape-shifter, someone who can become another creature – we Vikings believe in such things. Now turn yourself into a great eagle, take to the sky, and fly northwards. After a time, look below you, and what do you see?

A country with mountains sticking up through it like the half-buried bones of a dead giant. Forests of tall trees, shadows thick and dark beneath their branches. Ice glittering in the far north, where the white bears roam. Vast herds of reindeer moving slowly across the snowy wastes, with wolves in packs loping after them. Rocky beaches ruled by walruses and seals, whales spouting in the waves beyond.

These are the Viking lands, and living in them is hard. But tough lands breed tough people, and we have made these places work for us. Fly down, and you will see our farms, animals and crops. Touch the ground, and you are human once more…

Welcome to the steading I have always called my home.

These are the Viking
lands – living in them is hard

SCANDINAVIA: THE VIKING HOMELANDS

The Vikings came from the region now called
Scandinavia, in northern Europe. It's a huge territory,
but it was probably empty of people until after the last
Ice Age ended 12,000 years ago, when the early Stone-
Age hunter-gatherers arrived. The ancestors of the Vikings
probably came from the south – they were certainly related
to the other Germanic tribes that settled in northern Europe.

Another group came from the east. These were the **Sami**
people, who were a big influence on the Vikings.

The Greeks knew very little about Scandinavia, and the
Romans never conquered any part of it.

The Vikings burst on the world at the end of the eighth
century, when they started attacking other lands. For
the next 300 years they raided and traded and
fought all over Europe and the Middle East.
They gave Russia its name, settled in Iceland
and Greenland and were the first Europeans to
visit North America.

LIKE MOST Vikings, my family are farmers – everybody has to make a living from the land somehow. But there isn't much good land between the mountains and the sea, so we can only grow a few crops – oats, barley, rye. My family's land isn't too bad, so most years we grow plenty of vegetables – cabbages, peas and onions, and garlic and herbs to add flavour to our food. We have an orchard of apple and pear trees, but we also collect wild cherries and berries and nuts from the forest.

Sheep, goats and cattle give us meat, and we drink their milk and make butter and cheese from it. Pigs provide us with meat too, and we breed chickens for eggs and meat. We turn the wool from our sheep into clothes. We keep bees for their honey, and we brew strong mead from it to drink at our feasts, along with the ale that warriors love. Cattle-hides are good for shoe leather and belts, the reins and harnesses for our horses, the hand-grips of our swords and the coverings of scabbards.

We have always been hunters as well. Our lands are harsh, but they are full of wild animals we can hunt with the spear and the bow. Bears, boars, elk and different kinds of deer roam the woods, and there are many birds, especially ducks and other water-fowl. We eat their meat, and use their skins and feathers and fur to add to our clothes, and to keep us warm in bed through the long, cold nights of northern winters. We hunt wolves too sometimes, for their pelts and to protect our beasts. But our grey brothers and sisters always return. You can hear them howling at the moon.

Some of us also keep cats – they are very useful for making sure that no mice or rats get into our food-stores. Dogs are important to us too, both for hunting and for helping us with our flocks and herds – a well-trained, loyal dog is valued highly. We have many dogs on our steading, some of them the descendants of wolves… And we love birds of prey, the hawks and falcons we catch and train to hunt for us.

THE VIKING COUNTRIES

During the Viking Age, Scandinavia started developing into three countries.

SWEDEN is in the east. At the time of the Vikings it was mostly covered in forests, with many lakes, created by glaciers retreating at the end of the Ice Age and scraping holes in the ground. The country ("Sverige" in modern Swedish) is named after the **Svear**, a powerful tribe that lived there.

NORWAY is in the west facing the Atlantic. Its spine is a chain of mountains. It has a long coastline, full of amazing inlets from the sea, called **fjords**. The country was named Norway ("Norge" in modern Norwegian) for a simple reason: sailing along its coast was an excellent "way" for ships to get to the "north".

DENMARK is made up of the peninsula of Jutland and a large number of islands. Most of the land is flat, but in the Viking Age it was still hard to farm there. The country's name ("Danmark" in modern Danish) probably comes from two ancient words – "Dani" was the tribe that settled there and "mark" meant "border".

SOUTH OF DENMARK lived two peoples related to the Vikings, the Angles and Saxons. Their language was like Norse, the Viking tongue, and they worshipped the same gods. They became the **Anglo-Saxons**, who settled in Britain after the Roman Empire collapsed.

MAKE NO MISTAKE, our winters are *very* long and *very* cold. They are dark too, the days turning shorter until at midwinter there is almost no light, especially in the far north. Storms and blizzards bring thick snow to cover the land, and the lakes and rivers freeze. We have to stay inside for days at a time, only leaving shelter to make sure our beasts are safe and warm in their byres. Like most of us, I find that very hard, so it's good to get outside when I can. Long ago we learned from the Sami how to use wooden skis to get around, and we carve skates from the bones of animals to strap onto our shoes. I love the wild feeling of sliding down a slope on skis, the cold wind in my face, or skating on the glittering ice of a pond that has frozen solid.

Spring comes at last, the days getting longer and warmer. I always feel happier as the snow and ice melts – it's as if the world wakes up from a deep sleep. Then summer arrives, bringing heat and light, and things begin to grow – I love the feeling of that golden time. Darkness is banished, the days go on for ever, and we live outside as much as we can. We harvest our crops as the summer turns to autumn, the days become shorter, and soon cruel winter sweeps back with its darkness and cold.

There are many fish in the sea and lakes and streams that we catch with hook and line, or with nets. I think I might go fishing myself today... In the far north people hunt seals, walruses and whales, for their oil and blubber and bones as much as for their meat. The Sami people get most of what they need from their reindeer herds, although they often trade with us. They make many beautiful things from wood, animal bone and reindeer antlers – my father had a fine Sami knife with a carved handle that he always kept hanging on his belt.

The Sami are our brothers and sisters in the land, and we owe much to them.

THE SAMI PEOPLE

There are still many communities of Sami people living in northern Scandinavia and the far north of Russia to this day. Their origins were in the east, probably in the Ural Mountains area of Russia, and they were related to other peoples that

eventually settled in Finland, Estonia and Hungary. The Sami, Estonians and Hungarians speak related languages, all of them quite different to the tongue of the Vikings.

It's thought the Sami were far more widespread in Scandinavia during the Viking Age. The two peoples traded with each other, and married each other too. The Sami were partly nomadic, which meant they followed their reindeer herds. The Vikings learned a lot from them. There is evidence the Sami were good sailors as well as herders, and they may have taught the Vikings their boat-building skills.

Sami artefacts

The Sami believed everything in the world had a "spirit"
– people, animals and birds, even trees and rocks. They also
believed in magic and a supernatural world beyond ours.
They had priests called **shamans**, who spoke to the spirits and
performed rituals with chanting and drumming. The Vikings
absorbed some of this into the way they thought about the
world – especially the magic.

LIKE MOST VIKING farms, our steading has lots of buildings – byres and pens for animals, and barns for storage. But of course the most important is our longhouse.

A poor family's longhouse might be small, and a wealthy family's might be big. Of course, I think *our* longhouse is the best, far better than the longhouses of the richer farmers who live in other valleys near by. Our steading has always been the home of my family, of my father's father and his father before him, and others going back to the old times long before remembering. The people of my blood built this place and worked hard to make it good – and some of them died to protect it.

Our longhouse – my family's home

THE LONGHOUSE

Longhouses were similar across the whole Viking world. Some were built of logs, but turf or stone were also used if there was no wood. The roofs might be thatched, but often they were made of turf and covered with a layer of birch-tree bark. They sometimes had small windows, but it was usually smoky and dark inside, the only light coming from the hearth-fire and small lamps that burned fish-liver oil.

The inside was one large room, divided into several spaces. The hearth was in the middle of the hall, and the fire was kept going all the time – it provided heat for warmth and cooking, as well as light. There was a small hole in the roof where the smoke could escape. The floor was usually just earth trodden flat by everybody's feet.

There were benches along the walls for people to sit on, or to sleep on at night. In large halls there were often small side-rooms for tasks such as spinning and weaving, and so the lord and his family could have some privacy. There was not much furniture – a bed for the lord and his wife, chests to store valuable items. Big tables for feasts were kept stacked, and brought out when needed.

THE LONGHOUSE

"When I think of home, I see my parents sitting together on a bench by the hearth, smoke rising from the fire to the roof hole. A pot full of stew hangs above the flames..."

Shields on the walls

Roof-post

Beds

Smoke hole

Animal shelter – cows, sheep and goats were often kept inside, especially in the winter

Roof of turf or thatch

Hearth – the centre of the longhouse

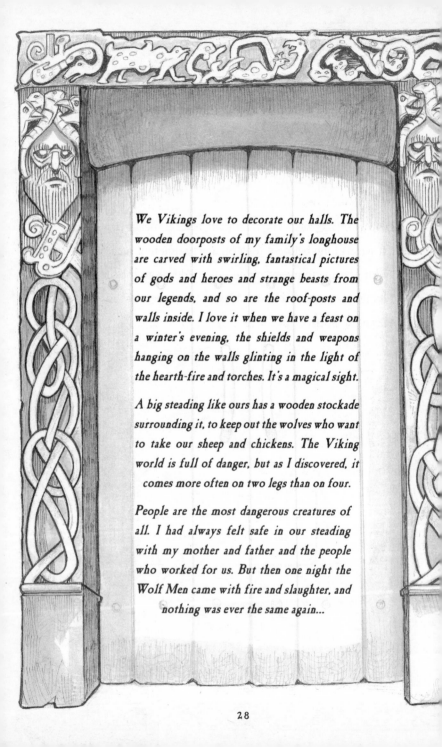

We Vikings love to decorate our halls. The wooden doorposts of my family's longhouse are carved with swirling, fantastical pictures of gods and heroes and strange beasts from our legends, and so are the roof-posts and walls inside. I love it when we have a feast on a winter's evening, the shields and weapons hanging on the walls glinting in the light of the hearth-fire and torches. It's a magical sight.

A big steading like ours has a wooden stockade surrounding it, to keep out the wolves who want to take our sheep and chickens. The Viking world is full of danger, but as I discovered, it comes more often on two legs than on four.

People are the most dangerous creatures of all. I had always felt safe in our steading with my mother and father and the people who worked for us. But then one night the Wolf Men came with fire and slaughter, and nothing was ever the same again...

People in other lands beyond the sea call us the Norse, or the Danes, if they know were we come from, or sometimes Men of the North, or Northmen. But they also call us Vikings, a name many of us are proud to bear. Some say it once meant little more than "men from the bays of Norway", and it's true that the word for "bay" in our Norse tongue is "vik". There is even a part of southern Norway called Viken. But whatever it meant to begin with, it wasn't long before it took on a very different meaning.

"Viking" came to mean "pirate", or "raider from the sea".

Viking is a name that strikes fear into our enemies, and makes them scan the horizon for the sails of our longships.

> *They are wise to be afraid, for we **Vikings** are not to be trifled with.*

TWO

STRONG MEN, TOUGH WOMEN

IT MIGHT COME as a surprise to people who only know us as terrifying raiders, but we Vikings are not all the same. In the Viking lands there are great differences between the rich and the poor. There are also those who are free, and those who are slaves. And there is a difference too, of course, between Viking men and women.

Viking men are the heads of their families, and much more. We build longhouses and longships, plough the fields and bring in the harvest. We are the craftsmen and hunters, the sailors and traders. We are warriors who fight to protect our families and friends, or in the wars of our lords. So a Viking man should be like my father – wise and clever and practical, and brave enough to face the battle-song of blades.

Viking boys are brought up to be strong and free and speak our minds, although we also learn to respect our elders. My father

made sure he taught me all the skills I would need to run a farm
when the time comes. He taught me to track game in the forest as
well. I felt proud when I made my first kill on a hunt, a wild boar
I took with a spear. I was only eight summers old at the time, and
I will never forget the sights and sounds of that day, the thrill and
fear of the chase, the smell of blood…

Learning how to hunt is one of the ways boys are taught how
to be warriors. You need strength and courage on the hunting trail
– a boar, a bear or a wolf will always fight for its life. You also need
weapon skills, both as a hunter and warrior. So our fathers teach
us the use of weapons from the day we can walk. My father was
a great warrior and he taught me all about handling axe, spear,
sword and shield.

VIKING ARTS AND CRAFTS

The Vikings were highly skilled at working with metal and wood, and at weaving. They liked to decorate what they made, whether it was a brooch or the dragon prow of a longship. With its swirling lines and convoluted pictures – often of animals, real or mythical – Viking art is very distinctive.

A rune stone

RUNES

The Vikings didn't have paper and pens or books, but they did have their own way of writing – their runes. These were simple letters that were easy to carve into wood, bone or stone. The Vikings used them to mark property, make lists, as inscriptions on memorials and tombs, and perhaps also in their religion and magic spells.

To begin with there were 24 letters in the rune alphabet. But in the early ninth century, at the time when the Vikings were beginning their raids overseas, they started using a shorter alphabet of only 16 characters. This was called the Futhark – the name is a combination of the first six letters – F, U, TH, A, R, K.

The Runic alphabet known as the Futhark

GIRLS AND WOMEN take a different path.

My mother Helga will explain…

"Men might build the houses, but it is we women who run their households, and our work is never done. We do the cooking and cleaning, we weave the cloth for everyone's clothes, then make them as well. So we have to be good at sewing and embroidery. We do our share of the farming too, usually taking care of the smaller crops, such as cabbages, peas and beans, and we make the butter and cheese.

"We give birth to the children and take care of them, and when our husbands are away trading or raiding, they leave us in

34

charge of everything. If our families are threatened, we will fight alongside our husbands, like a mother wolf protecting her cubs. That is why most Viking women will tell you that we are the equals of our menfolk, and in some ways even stronger than them.

"Girls are taught the skills they will need as Viking women. I learned from my mother how to help run a farm, how to make bread, butter and cheese, and how to spin and weave. I looked after the babies and younger children when she was busy, and learned that way how to be a mother myself. And I learned how to give as good as I got from the boys. Nobody was ever going to push *this* Viking girl around…"

VIKING WOMEN

Viking women had a lot of independence. They usually married between the ages of 12 and 15, but they could divorce their husbands. They were entitled to own property and even land.

There is evidence that Viking women were ready and willing to fight alongside their husbands. In the story of Gísli Sursson, one of the most famous Icelandic sagas, Gísli and his wife Aud stand back to back and fight off their enemies together.

There may even have been Viking women warriors. In a grave in Birka, Sweden, a warrior was found buried with Viking weapons. It was originally thought to have been a man, but a recent test revealed she was a woman.

How a Viking
woman warrior
may have looked

WE VIKINGS know how to have fun too. Our parents make toys for us when we are small – my father made me a toy sword and shield before I could walk! Viking children like to run and climb and play rough games, such as wrestling. Sometimes our games can be very rough – but that can help us learn how to be brave in defeat as well as in victory.

We have skating races on frozen rivers in winter, and running races in summer. I have always been good at both, and I win more often than I lose.

VIKING NAMES

*Personal names were very important for the Vikings. When children were born they were given first names that meant something. They were thought to give qualities to children that would help them in their lives. For example, the name **Gunnar** comes from two words in Norse – **Gunnr**, meaning war, and **Ar** meaning warrior.*

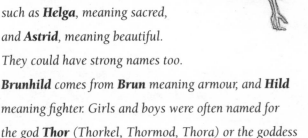

*Some names were based on animals – **Bjorn** meant bear, and **Ulf** meant wolf. **Orm** meant serpent or dragon. **Viglaf** comes from **Vig**, another word for war, and **Laf**, which meant "one who survives". Women had names such as **Helga**, meaning sacred, and **Astrid**, meaning beautiful. They could have strong names too. **Brunhild** comes from **Brun** meaning armour, and **Hild** meaning fighter. Girls and boys were often named for the god **Thor** (Thorkel, Thormod, Thora) or the goddess **Freyja**.*

*The Vikings didn't have surnames – instead they had **patronymics**. That means you are known as the daughter*

or son of your father. Gunnar's father was called Bjorn son of Sigurd, or **Sigurdsson**, and Gunnar was known as Gunnar **Bjornsson**. If Bjorn had a daughter called Thora, she would be known as Thora, daughter of Bjorn, or – in Norse – Thora **Bjornadottir**. This way of naming is still used in Iceland to this day, although some people choose to take their mother's name (a **matronymic**).

There could be lots of people with similar names, so the Vikings often gave each other **nicknames**. There were some excellent nicknames for women – **Unn the Deep-Minded** and **Sigrid the Haughty**, for instance. There were warriors called **Eirik the Victorious**, **Bjorn Ironside**, or **Thorfinn Skull-Splitter**. One was known as **Olvir the Child-Sparer** because, unlike some Vikings, he didn't kill children on raids.

But some nicknames were simpler. The Danish King **Sweyn Forkbeard** had a beard with a gap in the middle. His father was **Harald Bluetooth**, who might have had a tooth that was darker than the rest. **Harald Hardráda** or "hard-ruler" was a king of Norway. There was **Thord the Left-Handed**, **Ketil Flat-Nose**, **Thorstein Ill-Luck**, **Ulf the Squint-Eyed**. And **Eystein Foul-Fart** was clearly not very popular at all…

MY MOTHER and father taught me that it is good to be generous and welcoming to guests. They were great givers of gifts to their friends, and never turned anyone from our door. Travellers were greeted with food and drink, and could stay the night if they so wished. As my father often said, how can a man expect to be welcomed in the houses of others when he needs shelter, if he does not welcome them into his?

My parents also taught me that you should always try to look your best.

VIKING STYLE

Vikings wore tunics and trousers. Women wore dresses with a pinafore on top, fastened with a pair of oval brooches. Clothes were sometimes brown or grey, but the Vikings liked bright colours too, and used vegetable dyes to produce red, blue or yellow cloth. Rich Vikings wore embroidered clothes made of expensive cloth, even silk from distant lands.

Both men and women wore warm cloaks in cold weather, usually fastened with a brooch on the shoulder, and sometimes cloaks with hoods. Jewellery was popular. The Vikings

appreciated the value of gold, but they particularly loved beautiful things made of silver. Women wore finger-rings, necklaces and brooches, and a rich warrior might also carry his wealth on his arms in the form of large silver arm-rings.

Children generally wore the same kind of clothes as the grown-ups – boys dressed like smaller versions of men, girls like women. The Vikings looked after their hair, men as well as women – archaeologists have found lots of Viking combs. Men usually had beards, and there's evidence that tattoos were popular. It also seems the Vikings liked to keep themselves clean, and took a bath at least once a week.

WE HAVE FEASTS with much food and drink

at special times in the year – in the spring to welcome the good
weather, and in the autumn when we bring in the harvest. There
is an outdoor feast on Midsummer Night, and a hall-feast on
Midwinter Night, when we celebrate Yule Tide and pray for the
sun to return. In the long, dark winter nights we like listening
to poems and songs and old stories about heroes and the gods.
My favourite stories are those about great warriors and their
adventures. I like to hear about journeys and battles, and I wonder
if I would be brave in a storm of blades.

We have special games to play indoors as well. My favourite is
Hnefatafl…

HNEFATAFL

This means "King's Table" in Norse. It was a Viking board game similar to chess, with moveable pieces – a king, his defenders and attackers. It's for two players, each taking turns to move their pieces, and the aim is to capture the king.

Like chess, Hnefatafl was all about strategy, so it was thought that it helped boys learn how to win battles. But girls probably played it as well. The game was popular throughout the world of the Vikings until sometime in the eleventh century.

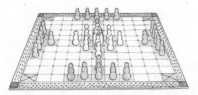

FINALLY I should tell you of the three classes of men among the Vikings. Ours is a world of men, so they matter most, although I know my mother doesn't agree…

I will speak of the rich first – we call them **Jarls**. They are men like my enemy, Skuli, rich in flocks and herds. Their halls are large and filled with their families and many servants. Such men often have wives from other rich families, and a band of warriors to do their bidding. A jarl might be rich in silver as well, and traders will fly to him like bees to honey, to sell him beautiful things from faraway lands.

Next come the **Karls**, men like my father; the farmers and warriors, traders and craftsmen such as blacksmiths, and their

Skálds   **Karls**

families. They are free, but not rich. Many farmers have their own steadings, but some might be tenants of a jarl and give him a portion of what they grow as rent. Warriors might swear an oath to serve a jarl, and traders and craftsmen earn their living by selling their goods or their skills.

Then there are the slaves, or **Thralls**. Some are slaves born to slaves, while others were once free. They might have been warriors defeated in battle, or people taken in a raid and sold at a slave market. Their masters have the power of life and death over them, and they are often made to work very hard. But good masters treat their slaves well, and slaves who save enough money can sometimes buy their freedom.

Jarl   Thralls

SLAVES OF THE VIKINGS

Slavery was an essential part of the Viking economy.

Archaeologists have found **thrall rings** – metal collars that slaves of the Vikings were forced to wear round their necks – and shackles and chains, just like those used later in history when Africans were taken to America.

There were slave markets in Viking towns such as **Hedeby** in Denmark and **Birka** in Sweden. But the biggest was in **Dublin**, a city founded by the Vikings. For several centuries many slaves from Britain, Ireland and further afield were sold there.

But however rich a jarl might be, and however brave a great hero, there are beings above us all who are far more powerful. It is time for you to meet our gods...

THREE
GODS AND MONSTERS

WE VIKINGS are a level-headed, practical people, and we live rooted in a world that is very real. I can see the high mountains behind our steading, and the leaden sky above them. I can smell the rich stew cooking in a pot over the hearth-fire, and taste its warmth and goodness in my mouth. I can feel the weight of my father's sword in my hand, and I can hear the wolves howling in the dark forest when night falls.

But we believe there are eight more worlds, making nine altogether. Perhaps that's why the number nine is a lucky number for us. Among them is the realm of our gods, the great, powerful beings who rule our lives. They are fierce and unforgiving, and they demand we keep them happy with our worship and the blood of sacrifices. Some people say that in an older time our ancestors sacrificed people. But these days we offer up a lamb or a goat, or perhaps – for something important – a fine bull.

We offer our gods the blood of sacrifices

We can worship our gods anywhere – in a forest grove, in the hall of a chieftain, in a god house built for that purpose, although we have no priests. We ask the gods to give us good luck at times of change and danger too, those moments when the doors between the worlds seem to open and we see that doom might be waiting – when a baby is being born, when someone falls ill, when a battle is about to begin.

There are many gods, yet often some people feel a close bond with just one. My father's chosen god was Thor, the great god of thunder. Father always wore an amulet round his neck to bring him luck, a small Hammer of Thor, and I carried it with me after he died. Yet Odin is the god for me, the one I worship above all. He found me at a time when I was lost and alone, and gave me help when I needed it most. But that is another story, one you can read for yourself...

Odin has many names, and he is the god of many things. We believe he is especially the god of war and poetry – great warriors are often great poets as well. The nine worlds are joined by the colossal ash tree we call **Yggdrasill**; all sorts of strange and wonderful creatures live in its realms – gods and people, elves and dwarves, ice giants and incredible beasts. But three of the worlds are more important than the rest.

At the top of the tree is **Asgard**, which means "world of the gods". That is where Odin and the other gods live. Below it is **Midgard**, which means "Middle Earth", the world of people.

These are connected by the great rainbow bridge called *Bifrost*, guarded by the god Heimdall. And at the very bottom lies **Niflheim**, the world of the dead. There a terrifying goddess called Hel rules a land that is always in darkness. Her top half is beautiful, but she is a hideous monster from the waist down…

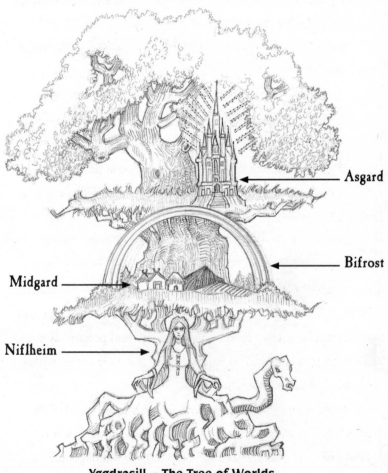

Asgard

Bifrost

Midgard

Niflheim

Yggdrasill – The Tree of Worlds

THE NORSE GODS

The Norse myths are full of stories about gods behaving like people. They fought and feuded and played tricks on each other, and just like the Greek gods, they enjoyed interfering in human lives.

ODIN: the greatest god. He was the father of many gods, and he created the human race, so he was also called the **All-Father**. He gave an eye to gain wisdom, and then he was hanged from **Yggdrasill** for nine days to suffer and learn even more. Odin was also called "Ygg", thought to mean "the terrifying one". "Drasill" means "horse", so the name **Yggdrasill** means something like "the steed of the terrifying one", a very poetic image of Odin "riding" **The Tree of Worlds**.

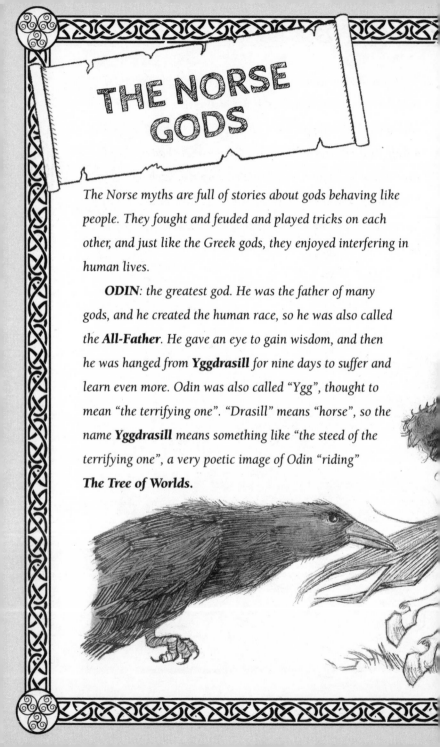

Odin always seems to crackle with menace and mystery in the stories. Odin visited Midgard in disguise, wearing a hat with a wide brim dipped over his empty eye socket. He carried a staff, or a magical spear called **Gungnir**. He had a pair of ravens who spied for him, one called **Hugin** (which means "thought") and the other called **Munin** (which means "memory"). If he wanted to get somewhere fast, he could always leap onto **Sleipnir**, his eight-legged horse.

THE NORSE GODS

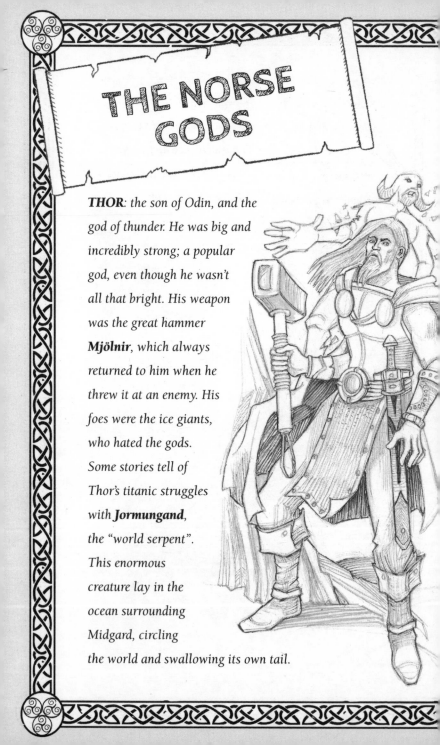

THOR: *the son of Odin, and the god of thunder. He was big and incredibly strong; a popular god, even though he wasn't all that bright. His weapon was the great hammer **Mjölnir**, which always returned to him when he threw it at an enemy. His foes were the ice giants, who hated the gods. Some stories tell of Thor's titanic struggles with **Jormungand**, the "world serpent". This enormous creature lay in the ocean surrounding Midgard, circling the world and swallowing its own tail.*

LOKI: *a major character in the Norse myths. He was a handsome mischief-maker, just like Anansi, the African trickster god. Loki was always plotting, and in one way or another he started most of the conflicts between the gods and with their enemies. His actions led to the death of Odin's favourite son, the beautiful* **Baldur**. *Strangely enough, Loki was also the father of several hideous creatures in the stories – the goddess Hel, Jormungand the world serpent, and the huge wolf* **Fenrir**.

THE NORSE GODS

There were of course several goddesses, although it seems the Vikings were more interested in male gods than female ones. **Frigg** was Odin's wife, and she plays a role in the story of Baldur. There was also **Freyja**, goddess of love and fertility and magic. She was said to have loved gold, and she had a legendary necklace called **Brisingamen** – which Loki stole. However, the names Frigg and Freyja are similar, and there's a theory that originally they might have been the same goddess.

THE GODS are great, of course, but as I found out, there is something greater; a force so powerful that not even Odin can resist it. Odin himself will explain...

"You speak of fate, Gunnar, the destiny of all things. You have seen the Norns for yourself, the weird sisters whose lair lies at the foot of great **Yggdrasill**. There in the darkness they weave the Web of Fate. The strands are the lives of everyone, and the Norns decide when each one will be cut, even those of the gods. But unlike you, we gods know exactly what doom awaits us at the end of time.

"One day the forces of darkness will rise against us and Asgard will be attacked by an army of giants, monsters and the dead. That is why I send my Valkyries to collect great warriors who die in battle and to bring them to me, to Valhalla in Asgard – I will need an army of my own to fight my enemies. Yet I know that we will lose, that our fate has already been decided by the Norns and there is no way to change Ragnarok..."

RAGNAROK
THE DOOM OF THE GODS

"Ragnar", the first part of the word, means "the gods". The second part, "ok", means "destiny" or "fate", although there's also a theory it might mean "dusk" or "twilight". But whether the whole word means "The Twilight of the Gods" or "The Doom of the Gods", the idea of **Ragnarok** *was still hugely important to the Vikings.*

Odin's **Valkyries** *were legendary women warriors who rode huge winged wolves and wore black armour and helmets that made them look like giant ravens. Their name means "Choosers of the Fallen" –* **Valhalla** *means "The Hall of the Fallen". The Vikings always said the first visitors to any battlefield once the fighting was over were the ravens and wolves, who came to eat the flesh of the dead warriors.*

In the Norse myths, the **Nornir** *are three weird women who speak in riddles and decide everyone's destiny. The idea of them weaving everyone's lives and fates is in their names – they're called* **Urthr**, *which means "the past",* **Verdandi**, *"the present" and* **Skuld**, *"the future". In the Greek myths, the three* **Moirai** *– the Fates – are similar to the Norns, as are the Three Weird Sisters in Shakespeare's great Scottish play* **Macbeth**. *Macbeth was a real Scottish king in the eleventh century, a time when the Vikings had settled all over Scotland.*

The Nornir

ANOTHER PART of our Viking belief is a
powerful magic called *Seithur*, something we have learned from
the Sami. It is used for predicting the future, healing the sick, and
darker things too, such as curses and spells to help warriors defeat
their enemies in battle. A woman who practises *Seithur* – it is
always women – is called a *Völva* in our tongue. She carries a staff,
can talk to the dead and to spirits, and falls into a trance to make
her magic. The *Völva* are shape-shifters as well.

A Völva

A Draugar

We know that people can come back from the dead too. Great warriors are often buried with their treasure in grave mounds, large chambers built with wood and stones, then covered in soil. Such a tomb is called a *Haugr*, and sometimes the corpse inside one comes back to life as a terrifying ghost called a *Haugbui*. Luckily it can't leave the mound, but it will certainly give any tomb robbers a nasty surprise.

There are also the *Draugar*, another kind of undead creature; people who die but refuse to stay buried. Unlike the *Haugbui*, the *Draugar* can leave their graves and return to their homes. In the stories about them they're always really bad-tempered and ravenously hungry. They gobble down every animal they meet – and people too, sometimes. They grow to an enormous size and are very difficult to get rid of.

NAGLFAR
THE SHIP OF DEAD MEN'S NAILS

*One of the strangest and most frightening things in the Norse myths is **Naglfar**, a ship said to be made entirely from the fingernails and toenails of dead men – "Nagl" was the Norse word for "nail", and "far" means "journey". At **Ragnarok**, the day of doom, the ship brings the dead from Hel's realm of Niflheim to attack the gods, with Loki steering it.*

SO THERE IS darkness and doom at the heart of what we Vikings believe. Surely that must lead to despair, you might say. You might even ask – if our fates really are foretold in this way, and there is nothing we can do to change them, why then do we bother to go on living? I remember putting that very question to my father.

"Because life is good, Gunnar, that's why! What does it matter that your fate is decided? The Norns know the day of your doom, but *you* don't – it could be today, or it could be many years from now. To be alive in this beautiful world with all its wonders is a great gift, so you had better make the most of it while you can. A true Viking understands that you should live your life well, and die well too."

THE VIKING DEAD

The Vikings laid their dead to rest in several different ways. Archaeologists have found many graves where men, women or children were buried, often with personal objects – weapons and armour for warriors, jewellery and coins, even toys.

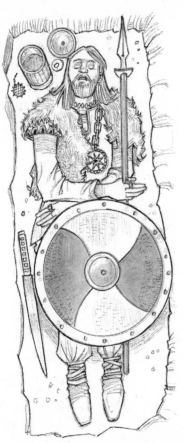

In some graves, the dead person has been laid on their side, with a pillow under their head, almost as if they're only sleeping. There's also evidence that the Vikings sometimes burned their dead on funeral pyres, with huge cremation ceremonies for important men and kings.

Great warriors were buried in mounds with their weapons, treasure, and animals that had been sacrificed, all to help them in their journey to the afterlife.

Sometimes important people were placed in longships that were then buried. One such ship was found at **Oseberg** in southern Norway. It was over 22 metres long and contained the bodies of two women, probably a powerful Viking queen and her slave.

Another longship was found in a mound in **Gokstad**, in southern Norway. It was over 24 metres long and contained the body of a tall man of about 60, almost certainly a great chieftain.

Although robbers had broken into both tombs, there was much for archaeologists to study. The reconstructed ships can be seen in the **Viking Ship Museum** near Oslo, the capital of Norway.

> My father knew what he was talking about. He was a man of honour who always spoke the truth. He lived his life fearlessly, and died with his sword in his hand, fighting to protect my mother and me. It was a great end for a great warrior. But there is much more to being a warrior, as you are about to find out.

FOUR

THE WAY OF
THE WARRIOR

LIKE MOST Viking boys, I always wanted to be a
warrior. Even when all I had to fight with was a wooden sword, I
dreamed of standing shoulder to shoulder with my shield-brothers
in the storm of battle. But I learned that war is not a game, and
that there is no place to hide when blades are singing and arrows
are raining from the sky. Only then will you know if you truly
have the courage to be a warrior – or not.

I was lucky that I had my father to teach me how to use
weapons. But thanks to Odin, I was also lucky enough on my
journey to encounter another battle-steeled warrior. My friend
Rurik has been on many raids, fought in great battles, and served
as one of the Greek Emperor's bodyguards in Constantinople,
which we call the Great City, or *Miklagard* in our tongue. He
knows more about fighting than any man.

"War is a simple business, Gunnar. You need to be fit and

strong, and to practise hard with your weapons so that they feel like a part of you. You need to be alert, to keep your eyes open in a fight so you can see what's coming – and you have to tame your fear. We all feel fear when we are fighting, even the best of us. Any man who tells you he does not is either lying to you or to himself, probably both.

"You need brave companions around you, men you can rely on when things get tricky. Such warriors would rather be killed than let down their shield-brothers – that would bring great shame upon them. But even greater shame awaits any man who swears to serve a chieftain, a jarl or a king and isn't willing to die for him. That is the bargain a warrior makes, and you boys should know it is not a life for everyone.

"If you can do all that, then you will win great glory and honour, and perhaps plenty more besides. But remember, a true Viking thinks nothing of riches, and never boasts of what he has done. You should treat victory and defeat as two sides of the same coin. And when the day of your doom arrives, make sure you die with a sword in your hand and laughter on your lips. Such is the way of the warrior."

Rurik

71

GOING DOWN FIGHTING

The Vikings admired courage and skill with weapons in a warrior, but to be truly great they believed you had to be cool and witty too. They loved stories of warriors who go down fighting against impossible odds, and die with a final joke on their lips to show defiance of their enemies and death itself. In some ways, the Vikings believed you could only tell a man's strength of character by how he dealt with defeat.

One story shows this perfectly. **Ragnar Lothbrok** *was a famous Viking in the ninth century. "Lothbrok" means "Hairy-Breeches", although nobody knows how he came by that name. After a violent, bloodthirsty career, Ragnar fell into the clutches of his greatest enemy, King Aelle of Northumbria. Aelle ordered him to be thrown into a deep pit filled with poisonous snakes. But Ragnar faced this terrible end with true Viking courage, and even composed a "death song" for the occasion.*

It's called **Krakumal***, which means "Crow Song" in Norse – crows were associated with death in Viking lore. In the song, Ragnar talks about all the fighting he's done, and how he has no complaints that the moment of his doom has come. Now*

he's looking forward to drinking ale with Odin in Valhalla, although he also says, "how the little piggies will grunt when they hear how the Old Boar suffers". He's saying his sons will come to take revenge on Aelle when they find out how he killed their father.

But best of all – at least from a Viking point of view – is the last line of the song, a terrific moment of defiance. In Old Norse it's

LAEJANDI
SKALK DEYJA!

which means:

LAUGHING
SHALL I DIE!

Historians have pointed out that it would have been hard to find enough poisonous snakes in Northumbria to fill a deep pit and kill a Viking. But even if it's not historically true, Ragnar Lothbrok's death is still a great story which tells us much about the mindset of Viking warriors.

THE DEATH OF RAGNAR HAIRY-BREECHES

TO BE A GOOD warrior you need good weapons and armour. Viking smiths are skilled, but getting kitted out for war can be costly; mail-shirts, iron helmets and swords are the most expensive items. So most Vikings fight instead with a spear or a small axe, and protect themselves in the battle-storm with a shield, a padded jerkin and cap.

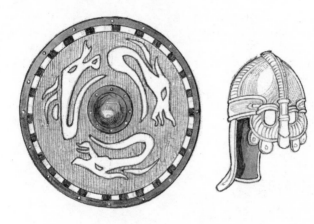

But a great warrior like Rurik in full war gear – a true lord of war – is a sight both memorable and terrifying – if you are his enemy...

A LORD OF WAR

AXE: *These came in a variety of sizes. Small axes were good for hacking at opponents, and for hooking over shields to pull them down. Big axes with wooden shafts of up to 2 metres were powerful weapons, but both hands were needed to wield one.*

HELMET: *Made of solid iron, often with a faceplate to protect the nose and eye area, but sometimes with just a nose-piece. A jarl or a king might have a helmet engraved with pictures of Odin or Thor, a fierce beast or a monstrous creature.*

SHIELD: *Made of wood with an iron rim and a "boss" in the middle. Some Vikings painted their shields in bright colours or with pictures of mythical beasts. Mainly protective, but could also be used as a weapon to strike an opponent.*

MAIL-SHIRT: *Made of hundreds of tiny iron rings linked together. Protected wearer from being slashed by swords, particularly if worn with a padded jerkin under it. Less effective at stopping spear thrusts, and heavy, so wearers needed to be strong.*

SPEAR: *At least 2 metres long, with a shaft of ash wood and an iron, leaf-shaped blade. Good for thrusting and keeping an opponent at a distance. Could also be thrown to wound or kill, or to stick in an opponent's shield, making it hard to use.*

SWORD: *A metre in length, the blade was sharp on both edges, with a shallow groove along it for flexibility (a rigid blade could break in a fight). Iron hand-guard, hand-grip covered in leather or cord, pommel for balance. Lethal at close quarters.*

BOW: *Good for harassing enemies and keeping them on the back foot before getting up close and personal, especially in the hands of a skilful archer. Arrows could penetrate mail-shirts, and barbed arrow-heads could inflict nasty wounds.*

MY FATHER told me about when his own sword was forged…

"It takes a great smith to make a great sword, and such men are never short of work. The smith heats nine rods of the best iron till they glow white, then beats and welds them together, doing the same over and over again. After a while they take on the shape of a sword, yet still the smith works at it, hammering, polishing. Eventually he dips it one last time in icy water, and out of the hissing steam comes a raw blade bearing a faint pattern; a weave of wavy lines, the ghosts of those iron rods.

"The smith adds a hand-guard and a pommel and binds the grip. There is sword-magic too, sometimes… A *Völva* chants a spell that will give the sword great power, and the smith carves her words in secret runes on the blade. Only then does he sharpen it with a whet-stone on both edges. Finally he makes a scabbard, from wood lined inside with sheep-fleece – the oily wool keeps the blade free from rust.

"Such a sword is said to be greedy for blood. Each kill feeds it, and makes it eager to kill again. My own father – your grandfather, Gunnar – passed his sword on to me. He was a mighty warrior, the scourge of his enemies in many battles, so now when I pull it from the scabbard it feels like a living creature in my hand, one that will slice through my foes like a scythe through standing barley. That's why its name is *Death-Bringer*."

VIKING SWORD MAGIC

Vikings believed swords had a kind of dark magic power, especially old swords that had been used in battle by famous warriors. Some swords were passed on from father to son, or from a jarl to a favoured warrior among his men. Many were buried with their owners – archaeologists have found swords in hundreds of Viking graves.

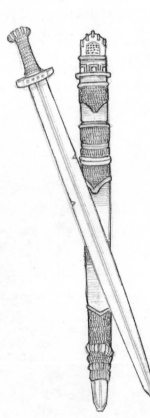

The Vikings gave their swords names, such as **Leggbitr** (Leg-Biter), **Naegling** (Hole-Maker), **Gunnlogi** (Battle-Flame), **Skrofnung** (Gnawer). King Olaf of Norway called his sword **Hneitr**, which means "Cutter". And in **The Saga of the Volsungs,** the mythical hero Sigurd kills the dragon Fafnir with his sword **Gram**, and that just means "Fierceness" or "Anger".

MY FATHER and Rurik taught me the art of fighting man-to-man, of staying light on my feet and watching an opponent's eyes rather than his blade. They also taught me the art of fighting in a shield-wall, which is harder than it looks. The warrior on your right defends you with his shield, while you do the same for the man on your left, and so on all the way down the line. You have to make sure all the shields overlap.

We learn to trust each other, and that is why we talk of being shield-brothers. There is nothing as terrifying as the storm of battle, that moment when two shield-walls crash, blades sing, blood flows and warriors die. So there is no bond as strong as that between men who have stood together and lived to tell the tale. Although there are warriors who leave the shield-wall to fight alone, the ones we call *berserkers*.

Learning to fight man-to-man

81

BERSERKER MADNESS

Berserkers were terrifying

We get the word **berserk** from the Vikings. **Berserkers** were a kind of warrior who fell into a trance in battle and behaved as if they couldn't be wounded by ordinary weapons.

They were said to strip off their armour and tunics and fight almost naked – **ber** could have meant "bare" and **serk** probably meant "shirt". But some historians think it meant they fought in **bearskins**, taking on the spirit of the creature.

Berserkers were terrifying – often covered in tattoos and with their teeth filed to sharp points like a wolf's. They were said to bite their shield-rims in their impatience to get a battle started, and didn't care if they lived or died. Berserkers weren't always popular with their own side; when the true berserker madness descended upon them they were just as likely to attack their fellow warriors as their enemies.

Needless to say, the average Viking berserker didn't live long.

> There is no doubt that we Vikings are very good at war. We knew it, of course, but the peoples of other lands didn't – they thought we were nothing but savages. They had no idea of the terrible doom that was heading their way.

FIVE
FIRE, BLOOD AND PLUNDER

WE COULD have stayed in our homelands for ever, living as our ancestors had done since the days before remembering. But the Norns crafted a different fate for us. There had aways been raiding between neighbours in our lands. Man is wolf to man, after all, and when times are hard the strong always take from the weak. Then something new started. Men decided to sail far across the sea to go raiding. Perhaps some had grown tired of trying to scratch a living from our hard lands, and longed for freedom and adventure instead. Perhaps others were younger sons who lost out to their brothers when it came to inheriting the family farm after their father had died. Young men often grow restless, and may seek ways of winning fame and fortune. Or perhaps it was simply that Odin decided he needed more warriors in Valhalla – raiding is dangerous for the raiders as well as for their victims.

One thing was certain, though – there was wealth for the taking in other lands. We had long traded with lands to the south and west, sending them furs and pelts, which they bought with their coins. The peoples of those lands were Christians, which meant they worshipped a god whose name was Christ. They did this in their god-houses – they called them churches – and prayed, but they made no sacrifices. Instead, they filled their churches with lots of gold and silver ornaments.

Then our traders began to talk of even richer steadings called monasteries, where many priests or monks lived together. The Christians often built them on the coast, which meant they were easy to reach across the sea. So it wasn't long before some among us laid plans to visit these places, and began to build the right ships for the voyage.

Riches raided from monasteries

VIKING SHIPS

A ferja

Scandinavia is surrounded by the sea, and the Vikings developed a wide range of boats to take advantage of it. There was the **ferja**, a small boat used for fishing and hunting whales or seals. A **byrding** was bigger, and was probably used for trading trips up and down the coast. Then there was the sturdy **knarr**, a cargo ship used for longer trading voyages. All were powered by a square sail or by oars.

But in the late eighth century a new type of vessel appeared, the **longship**. This was designed for war, and historians think it was like a new secret weapon. As the name implies, it was long and narrow, and it was fast, whether it was running before the wind with its large square sail or being rowed by its crew. It could voyage across the deepest ocean, yet it could also be landed on a beach or travel up a shallow river, swiftly penetrating right into the heart of a country. So a longship was the perfect vessel for making surprise attacks.

Longships were built

A byrding

A knarr

by master shipwrights and
craftsmen. They chose the
timber carefully, and
made the keel and
mast from whole
trees. Planks were
cut and held together
by iron rivets to
form the overlapping
strakes of the hull. A helmsman steered with a rudder called a
steer-board attached to the right of the ship. That's where we get
our word "starboard", as in a vessel's starboard, or right side.

There were no benches – the crew rowed while sitting on the
sea-chests they brought with them. They greased and wrapped
their weapons and armour and kept them beneath the deck
planking where they could get to them quickly. Their shields
were kept in racks along the ship's sides. The sails were made of
specially treated wool and flax, sometimes decorated with stripes
or just dyed a fierce red.

Longships varied in size. The smallest were called **snekke**,
which means "snake-ship", and had a crew of thirty Vikings.
Larger ships were called **drakkar**, or "dragon-ships", because
they had terrifying prows carved in the shape of dragons or other
mythical creatures. These were thought to give the ship magical
protection. Dragon-ships usually belonged to jarls, chieftains, or
kings and could have crews of a hundred or more warriors.

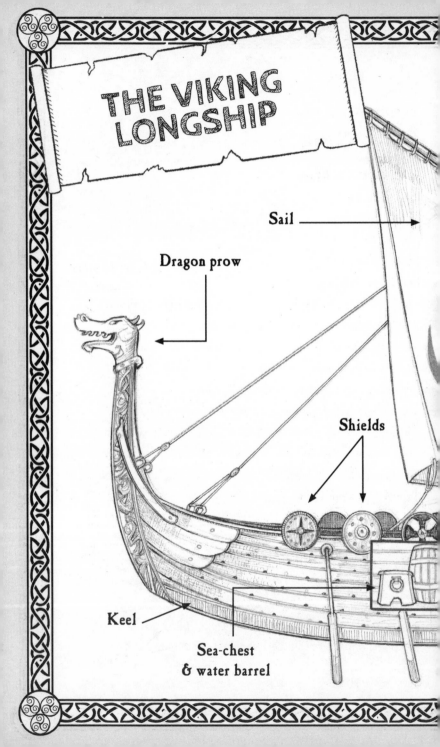

THE VIKING LONGSHIP

Sail

Dragon prow

Shields

Keel

Sea-chest
& water barrel

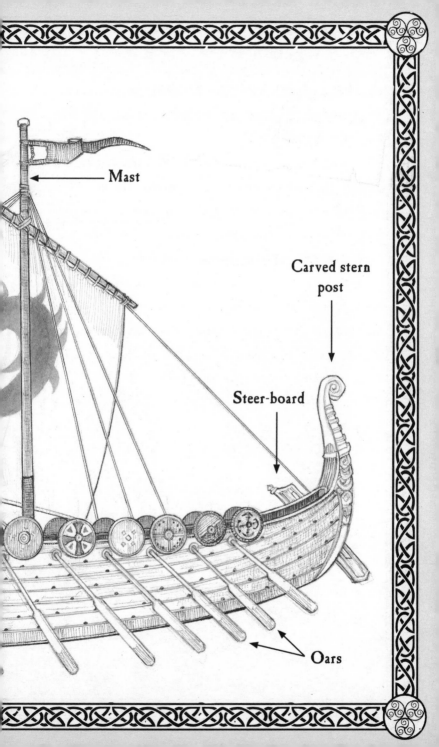

Mast

Carved stern post

Steer-board

Oars

A RAID is a terrible thing, full of fire and blood. I can hardly bear to think of the night the Vikings called the Wolf Men attacked our steading.

I encountered Viglaf on my journey. He is the skipper of the longship *The Sea-Eagle*, and he has led his crew of Vikings on many raids. So I will let him explain how they're done… "The secret of a successful raid is … surprise! I mean, if they don't know you're coming, they can't get ready for you. We're good at fighting, of course, but why take a risk if you don't have to? The best thing is to row in at night, beach the ship where it can be hidden – then make a stealthy approach at dawn. I make my lads stay silent and wrap their weapons in sheepskins so there's no chinking to give us away.

"Once you get started, you need to be ruthless. You have to

cut down anyone who stands against you, and find out where they're hiding their gold and silver, with a little bit of persuasion if necessary. They don't have much in most steadings, so we might take some of their livestock if we can get them onto the ship. We don't raid bigger steadings, those that belong to chieftains or lords – that can be very risky.

"Monasteries are our favourite places for plunder. The monks usually give up quickly and tell us where they've hidden their treasure. If they don't, they're easy to kill – it seems their god forbids them to fight back. We often find the treasure anyway. We keep some monks alive to sell as slaves. You can get a pretty good price at the Dublin slave market for a young monk who's used to hard work."

THE FURY OF THE
NORTHMEN

*The first Viking raid on Britain happened in 793CE. In the early summer of that year a band of Vikings raided the great monastery of **Lindisfarne**, on Holy Island in the Kingdom of Northumbria. They arrived from the sea with no warning, then seized whatever*

treasures they could lay their hands on. They burned the buildings, killed some monks, took others to sell as slaves and sailed off with their plunder.

More raids followed, on rich monasteries such as those at **Jarrow** and **Iona**, and all over Britain and Ireland. Priests soon began church services with a special prayer – *"Oh Lord, protect us from the fury of the Northmen."* But their prayers were no protection against the Vikings. Raiding became a very successful way of life for them. Over the next fifty years they raided constantly in Britain, Ireland and beyond.

Vikings raid the great monastery of Lindisfarne

RAIDING CHANGED things in our

homelands too. You soon heard about men who were doing well from raids. If they gained a reputation as brave and bold leaders, then warriors would seek them out, eager to join their crews and share in the plunder. A skipper might start raiding with just one ship and a small crew, but might end up with three ships or even more, with many men at his bidding.

We Vikings also like our leaders to be clever; courage is enough for the shield-wall, but often you need guile to get you out of trouble. They should be generous too, the kind of men we call *ring-givers*. A skipper who rewards his crew with silver arm-rings will never be short of followers, and is on the path to becoming a chieftain or jarl.

Such a man will build himself a fine hall, marry a wife from a rich family, and fill his fields with crops and his byres and pens with cattle and sheep. He will still go raiding in the summer, but in winter he will stay at home, feasting with his warriors. And he will make sure at least one of them is a *skáld*, a poet who can tell the old stories of gods and heroes to help the long, dark nights pass more quickly.

I have seen myself how a skáld can cast a spell over a crowded hall as he spins his tale. But a skáld with his wits about him knows he must also praise his lord…

A skáld casts a spell
over a crowded hall

WARRIOR POETS

The Vikings loved clever word-play and poetry. They didn't write things down until a lot later, after the Scandinavian countries began to become Christian in the 11th century. Runes were used for short inscriptions on personal possessions or stone memorials. Up till then all Viking myths and stories had to be learned by heart to pass them on, and that was easier if they were in the form of poems.

So for a long time all the stories about Odin, Thor, Loki, the Norns and the great heroes of the past came in the form of poems to be spoken. They were probably recited on special occasions such as sacrifices, and at feasts to entertain everyone. But the Vikings also made up new poems, and if you were good enough at doing that you might become a **skáld**; a man who made a living out of composing poems and reciting them in the hall of a chieftain, jarl or king. Of course the best way to earn plenty of arm-rings in such a job was to keep saying in your poems that your lord was incredibly handsome and brave – and very generous.

Skálds were expected to be good warriors, and warriors

were expected to be good poets. Some were good at being both. **Egil Skallagrimsson** was a bloodthirsty, violent Viking. He was captured by his greatest enemy, **King Eirík Bloodaxe of Jorvik**, who threatened to cut off Egil's head. But Egil wrote a praise-poem (**Höfuðlausn**, or "Head Ransom") for his captor that was so good Eirík decided to let him go. Skálds also wrote poems insulting their enemies; sometimes a couple of skálds would have a contest to see who could come up with the best insults, like rappers today.

A skáld contest

HEITI AND KENNINGS

Viking poetry was complicated and difficult to compose. It was based on very precise rules and is full of rhyme and alliteration. But what makes it particularly hard is the way it uses poetic words, or **heiti**, as well as **kennings**, special images that are often based on myths.

So instead of the word **ship** in a poem, you might say **keel**, using one part to describe the whole. A **horse** becomes a **steed**, and each of Odin's many names can be used as a heiti for him. Kennings have two parts, so a kenning for a ship might be **stallion of the sea**, which gives you a strong image of a ship as a living creature. **Death** is **sleep of the sword**, and **crimsoner of the wolf's jaws** is a **warrior**, who leaves the bodies of his enemies on the battlefield for scavenging wolves to eat.

It gets a lot more tricky when you mix in myth-based kennings – to understand them you have to know the myth. For example, **The Hanged God** is **Odin**. But a kenning for **gold** is **Sif's hair**. That's because Sif is Thor's wife, and there's a story about Loki cutting off her beautiful golden hair. The best skálds were thought to be those who could pack as many heiti and kennings into their poems as possible.

Here are some more kennings, and an example of what a Viking poem was like:

- **Storm of blades:** battle
- **Wound-sweat, corpse-dew:** blood
- **Battle-snake, bane of the shield, blood-wand, warrior's doom:** sword
- **Ring-giver, gold-giver:** generous chieftain or lord
- **Feeding the eagles:** killing your enemies in battle
- **Raven's harvest:** the dead on the field of battle
- **Whale's road:** the sea
- **Praise-smith, word-smith, word-weaver:** skáld (poet)
- **Sky-candle:** the sun

EGIL
A VIKING POEM

Smooth-tongued word-weaver,
Went on the whale's road,
Bound in a storm of blades,
Egil's battle-snake biting,
Wound-sweat scattered,
Shield-bane to his enemies,
A fine harvest for the ravens!

Yet raids are not the only way a Viking can win fame and fortune. We discovered there were lands to be settled far across the western sea, and riches waiting in the East...

SIX
SAILING THE WHALE'S ROAD

WE HAVE ALWAYS known of other lands across the great sea that stretches to the West and North, beyond Britain. A long while ago some families settled in the Faeroe Islands, a week's sailing west of Norway. They soon scared off the few Irish monks who were the only people living there. Now the sons and daughters of those families have farms with fine halls, and large flocks and herds that bring them wealth.

But in the early years of raiding we began to hear of a land of ice and fire to the North-West. A Norwegian called *Floki Vilgerdarson* set off to look for it, sailing the whale's road, as the skálds say. He wasn't impressed with the large island he found. It was cold there, and the land was covered in snow and ice, so he called it *Iceland*. But the men of his crew thought it looked like a place worth settling.

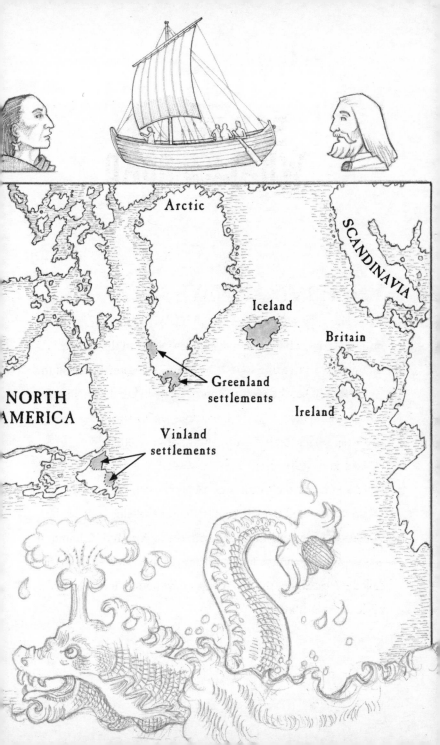

VIKING NAVIGATION

We don't know exactly how the Vikings navigated. On short voyages they must have stuck to the coast and looked for well-known landmarks. They were expert sailors, so they knew a lot about the tides, sea-currents and weather, and how long a voyage should take. If they lost sight of land they could find it again by following birds, or by checking the colour of the sea – it might be stained by mud from a river.

Voyages across the open sea were much harder. It could take three weeks to sail from Norway to Iceland even in good weather. They could work out roughly where they were by the positions of the sun and stars, and might even have used a simple sundial as a kind of compass. But they must also have got by on guesswork and prayers to Odin and Thor.

The northern seas could be terrifying and dangerous when the weather was stormy and the waves were icy. Only the brave and bold set out on the whale's road, especially if they were taking their families to settle in a new land.

PEOPLE FROM NORWAY started

moving to Iceland. Many were looking for good land to farm, but others wanted to get away from *Harald Harfágri*, or Finehair, a jarl who wanted to make himself king of all Norway. Some chieftains thought they would have more freedom in a new land and Harald was happy to see them go.

Things had been getting hard for raiders, too. The peoples of many lands had grown tired of being raided and had learnt to fight back, defending themselves and killing Viking raiders. According to Viglaf, the quickest way to get your head cut off was to be captured by a bunch of angry villagers.

Raided villagers had learnt to fight back

A NEW COUNTRY: SETTLING IN THE LAND OF ICE AND FIRE

A Norwegian called **Ingólfr Arnason** was the first Viking settler in Iceland. He had good reason to find a new home – he had killed a man and wasn't very popular in Norway any more. He landed in Iceland in 870CE, and founded a farm at a place he called **Reykjavík**. It means **Smoky Bay** in Norse – hot springs there produced a lot of steam. Over the next fifty years up to 20,000 more settlers and their slaves followed, coming from Norway and Viking settlements in Britain and Ireland.

They found themselves in a strange land of hot springs and geysers, glaciers, active volcanoes and regular earthquakes – with no inhabitants. The only good land to farm was around the coasts, and the climate was harsh. The Arctic Circle runs just to the north of Iceland, so the winters are long, dark and very cold.

But the settlers were hardy, and they soon carved out farms for themselves all round the island. They raised sheep and cattle for milk, cheese and meat, and fished to add variety to their diet. There were no towns or even villages, only individual farms, many in isolated parts of the island. Icelanders liked it that way; freedom was important to them right from the beginning.

Icelanders resisted the idea of having a king, but they did have powerful chieftains called the **Godar**. A **Godi** was a rich farmer who controlled a particular area, and had other farms that he rented out. They arranged marriages for their sons and daughters with other rich farmers, and ran things for their own profit. Some were also traders and travellers who visited the Viking homelands and other lands.

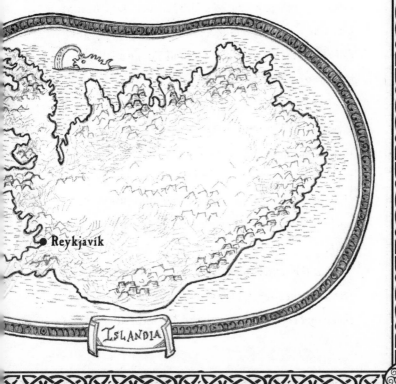

A NEW COUNTRY: SETTLING IN THE LAND OF ICE AND FIRE

However, there were plenty of disputes. Icelanders were fond of arguing with each other, about almost anything – lost sheep, a family inheritance, or perhaps just a remark seen as an insult. Viking men were quick to take offence – that was the dark side of the warrior code. Killings were common, and a

short argument could become a blood feud that lasted years.

The answer was to develop laws to deal with such problems, usually involving compensation. A victim's family might accept a payment – a blood price set according to the crime – rather than carry on a feud. If that failed, the case could be taken to the **Thing**, a regular meeting of the people in a district. Once a year people from all over Iceland met at the **Althingi,** a much bigger festival with a **Law-Speaker** who recited the law. In many ways the Althingi was like a parliament that governed Iceland.

BUT WE VIKINGS are restless by nature, and finding one new land was not enough. Travellers from Iceland journeyed further across the sea, almost to the edge of the world where *Jormungand* the World Serpent awaits. I have heard the stories they told about such men, but my old ship-mate and shield-brother Thorkel actually knew them: "If it's Eirík the Red you mean, Gunnar, I knew him well, and his son Leif the Lucky. Eirík was born in Norway, but his father Thorvald had to move the family to Iceland because he'd killed a man. Eirík was ten at the time. He got his nickname because of all the blood he spilt when he grew up – like father, like son. Eirík also killed a few men, and had to seek out a new home.

Eirík the Red discovers Greenland

"There had been talk of a mysterious land in the West, so Eirík went off in his ship to take a look. He found a huge, barren land, endless rock covered in mountains of ice, but came at last to a place that seemed promising. Eirík knew he'd need others to help him settle there, so he went back to Iceland to persuade people to join him. Being crafty, he called the new country *Greenland* to make it sound good.

"We should have called him Eirík Silver-Tongue, because his plan worked. He set off with a fleet of twenty-five *knarrs* full of families and their possessions and beasts. They sailed into bad weather, and only fourteen ships made it to Greenland. I heard some people weren't too happy with Eirík when they saw their new home. But they were Vikings, so they got on with it and started building farms for themselves.

"Eirík was right, though. Within a few years the settlements in Greenland were doing well. They traded with Iceland, and Eirík grew rich – some say he had as many as forty cattle! He was still grumpy, but he was too old to kill anybody by then. Too old to go travelling, as well. There was some talk of yet another mysterious land to the south-west, but it was Eirík's son Leif who went there...

"People called him Leif the Lucky because he always seemed to do well for himself and his family. He certainly had a real adventure in the place he called Vínland..."

VÍNLAND
THE VIKINGS IN NORTH AMERICA

In 986CE, a young Icelander called **Bjarni Herjólfsson** returned from a trading trip to Norway only to discover his parents had gone to Greenland with Eirík the Red. Bjarni set off to follow them, and his ship was blown off course. He saw a new land of hills and thick forest to the west, and his crew wanted to land there. But Bjarni was worried about getting lost, and steered the ship back onto its original course.

He did tell everyone about the new land they'd seen, though, and years later, in 1000AD, Eirík's son Leif decided to go there. Iceland and Greenland had few trees, and he thought he could make a profit by bringing back timber. Because grapes grew on wild vines there, he called it Land of the Vines, or **Vínland** in Norse.

In fact Leif and his companions had arrived in the continent that was later to be called **North America**. They were almost certainly the first people from Europe to do so, beating Columbus by nearly 500 years. Leif led several expeditions to Vinland, hoping to settle there. In the 1960s archaeologists discovered a Viking settlement at a place called **L'Anse Aux Meadows** in Newfoundland province, Canada.

Vinland did not last long, however, perhaps just a few years. The main problem was conflict with Native American tribes. According to the story – as told in the **Vinland Sagas** – to begin with the Vikings got on well with the **Skraelings**, as they called the Native Americans they met. But there was trouble that led to fighting and killings on both sides, and soon the settlement was abandoned.

VÍNLAND
THE VIKINGS IN NORTH AMERICA

One female character who stands out in the Vínland Sagas
is Gudrid Thorbjornadottir, also known as **Gudrid the Far-
Travelled**. She grew up in Iceland, then settled in Greenland with
her first husband. When he died, she married Leif Eiríksson's
brother **Thorstein**. They went to Vínland, but he died too. She
finally married a man called **Thorfinn**, and their son was the first
European born in North America. When she became a widow
for the third and last time she became a Christian and went on a
pilgrimage to Rome, where she met the Pope!

ICELANDERS ARE KNOWN to be

great travellers, of course, and they seem to turn up everywhere. Rurik says he met plenty of them on his wanderings in the East. Some were even in the Greek Emperor's bodyguard in Miklagard. The sun is often very hot there, and it's a long way from the icy North. But the Icelanders didn't mind, and they're great storytellers, so their shield-brothers liked having them around.

> The best skálds are Icelanders. Rurik thinks that's probably because they have nothing better to do in their frozen homeland but feud and make up poems...

THE ICELANDIC SAGAS

In the Viking Age, Icelanders had a reputation for being good storytellers and brilliant poets. They already had the Viking tradition of storytelling and word-play, but as settlers in a new land they wanted to preserve their myths and the legends of the distant past. They wanted to tell the stories of their struggles to survive – and their conflicts with each other.

Around 1000CE the Icelanders became Christians and stopped worshipping the old gods. Christianity brought the Bible with it, and some Icelanders learned to read and write, especially those who became priests or monks. Most of what they read was in Latin, the language of the Church. But the Icelanders were proud of their own language and stories, and over the next two centuries they wrote them down.

They called their stories **sagas,** which comes from the word **segja** and simply means "to say", revealing their origins as tales to be "spoken". There are three main groups of sagas – myths and legends, histories of the kings (mostly of Norway), and stories about the settlers of Iceland and their families. It's hard to know if the stories are entirely true, but they do tell us a huge amount about the Vikings.

The sagas feature feuds and conflicts between powerful men, with lots of voyages and fighting and snappy Viking dialogue. There are great characters such as **Egil**, the ugly warrior-poet (in **Egil's Saga**) and **Njal**, who comes to a fiery end (in **The Saga of Burnt Njal**). Egil's daughter **Thorgerd** is a tough character – her son Kjartan is murdered (in **The Saga of the People of Laxardal**) but she makes sure that he is avenged.

But places like Iceland and Greenland weren't for everybody, and plenty of Vikings didn't want to settle in either. Raiding had become more difficult, so there was only one other thing to do: they could become kings, or they could die trying.

SEVEN
KINGDOMS FOR THE TAKING

TO THE EAST of our homelands there is another, smaller sea that you can sail across in a few days. Beyond it lies a vast country of dark forests and great rivers and strange, wild tribes. Swedish Vikings have been raiding and trading there for a long time, leaving the West for the Danes and us Norwegians. There is much gold and silver to be had in the East, and plentiful adventure for a young Viking, as Rurik will explain…

"I grew up in the lands of the Svear, so I often heard tales of the East. People talked of Miklagard too, and it sounded like just

the place for me. So as soon as I was old enough to pull a longship oar I joined the crew of a good skipper, and set off to make my name. But even then I wasn't particularly interested in wealth. I wanted to be a warrior, win honour and glory in battle, and maybe see some wonders as well.

"I saw plenty on that first journey, and on the others I made later. The rivers are like enormous roads that take you first to the Kingdom of Cities, or *Gardariki* as we call it in our tongue. These are the Viking strongholds, places such as *Holmgardr* – the locals call it *Novgorod*. People from everywhere meet there, to trade furs and slaves. Some come from so far away that nobody has heard of their homelands.

"You can't get all the way south on a single river. So you go as far as you can, then haul your ship out of the water and move it on log rollers overland to the next river. It's hard work, and it is a dangerous time in the journey – there's a chance you might be ambushed. The tribes love to attack the *Rus*, as they call us. We have names for them too, the kind you use to curse someone who is shooting arrows at you…"

THE WILD EAST

Baltic Sea

Slavic tribes

Volga river

Dnieper river

Caspian Sea

Black Sea

Constantinople (Miklagard)

BYZANTINE EMPIRE

Swedish Vikings started exploring the lands east of the Baltic long before raiding began in the West. They built trading posts and forts which became important cities, and ruled the regions around them. The word **Rus** probably comes from a Finnish word – **Ruotsi** – that means a crew of oarsmen. It became the root of the name still used for those lands – **Russia**.

The most powerful of the Rus cities in the ninth century was **Novgorod**. Its first, half-legendary ruler was actually called **Rurik**. There weren't many Rus, probably just small bands of Vikings who ruled the local people. There were many different tribes, but most were Slavs, who became the Russians. Our word "slave" is derived from the word "Slav" for a simple reason – many Slavs became slaves. After a while the Vikings stopped speaking Old Norse and spoke early Russian instead.

The northern Rus were great travellers and traders, and made contact with the peoples of central Asia and the Islamic world of the Middle East. **Islam** was only a few centuries old, but the Vikings saw the Arabs as good trading partners. Many Vikings made fortunes from this trade and travelled as far as the Caspian Sea and Baghdad. Arab coins called **dirhams** are often found in Viking graves.

The Vikings loved to go travelling. There are many **rune-stones** in Scandinavia – stone monuments carved with runes – that record their journeys. It's possible some Vikings might even have been to both Vínland and Baghdad in their lifetimes.

"AFTER A FEW WEEKS you come to the great city of Kiev, another Rus stronghold. The ruler there is Oleg. He is a hard man, and he has carved out quite a realm for himself in the south-lands. You can't pass through Kiev without paying him a tribute, so make sure you have enough gold or silver. And don't think you'll get any special treatment because you're a Viking. The Kiev Rus are more than halfway to being Slavs.

"Next you come to another sea, and another week's sailing southwards brings you to Miklagard. I will never forget my first sight of its beautiful white buildings, the domes and towers of its churches, its narrow streets and wide roads packed full of people. I grew to know it as well as any man born there, and it was my proudest day when I took my place in the front rank of the Emperor's Varangian Guard."

"I will never forget my first sight of Miklagard's beautiful white buildings" -Rurik

THE VARANGIAN GUARD

The Vikings called the city Miklagard in Norse, but the Greek inhabitants called it **Constantinople**, which means "the city of Constantine". He was the Roman Emperor in the early fourth century, and he founded the city after he defeated his rivals and gained supreme power. By then the Roman Empire was split into two halves, and Constantinople became the capital of the eastern, Greek-speaking half.

The western half collapsed in the late fifth century, barbarian invaders creating new countries from its provinces. Yet the eastern half survived and prospered for another thousand years. The Vikings were dazzled by Constantinople's size and the city's obvious wealth, so they tried their usual raiding tactics. The city was too strong and they were defeated – but they impressed the Greeks with their fighting skills.

The Emperors offered the Vikings the chance to work for them as soldiers. The Vikings who took the job swore to serve the Emperor, and the Norse word for "oath" is "varar", so they were called **Varangians**. They were very well paid, and they got to travel a lot. The Empire controlled a large part of the

Eastern Mediterranean and was almost constantly at war, so the Varangians had to fight in many places.

They soon gained a reputation as ruthless warriors. It also meant they had plenty of opportunities to do some looting. **Harald Hardráda** was a Varangian for many years. He fought all over the Empire, and even visited Jerusalem. When he left at last he sailed for home with a ship full of gold and silver, which he used to help him become King of Norway.

Being a Varangian wasn't always exciting. The Empire was Christian, and the Emperor often went to church. As his bodyguards, the Varangians had to go with him. The main church in Constantinople was the cathedral of **Hagia Sophia**, and in one gallery there's some Viking graffiti. Two Varangians called Halfdan and Arni must have been bored – they carved their names in the marble, as you can see:

It's likely some Varangians were impressed by the wealth and power of Christianity in Miklagard and became Christians themselves. The religion certainly spread into the lands of the Rus in its Eastern Orthodox form, which is different from the Catholic variety in the West. There was a split between eastern and western Christians in the Viking Age. The Varangians who went home probably took the religion with them.

THERE WERE FORTUNES to be

made in the West too. We Norwegians settled in the Shetland Isles as we did in the Faeroes, and we made the Orkneys a Viking jarldom. From there we spread south to the lands of the Gaels – to Sutherland and Caithness in Scotland, and then to the Western Isles. We built strongholds in Ireland, towns such as Limerick and Cork. We conquered the Isle of Man, and controlled the Irish Sea.

There was a Viking chieftain called Hrolf the Walker – *Ganger-Hrolf* in Norse – because he was very big and no horse could carry him. He raided the Franks so often their king offered to give him lots of land if he would stop. Hrolf agreed, and settled down with his followers. The Franks called him Rollo, and that part of their country became known as the Land of the Northmen, or Normandy in their tongue.

But even bigger prizes lay just across the sea from Normandy, in the realms of the Angles and the Saxons. Some ambitious Vikings grew tired of just being raiders and began to wonder if there might be kingdoms for the taking. Such a man was my enemy, Skuli Eyjolfsson. At the end of my *Viking Boy* journey I fought him, and I sent him to Valhalla. But here I have summoned him from his tomb as an undead *haugbui*, so he can tell you about those wars himself:

"A few of us chieftains and jarls got talking, and we realized we'd do better if we worked together. Fighting off a raid by a single crew is one thing, but it's much harder when there are fifty

I have summoned Skuli from his tomb
as an undead haugbui

longships packed with warriors. Soon we were unstoppable, and
the Angles and Saxons started paying us to leave them alone.
Of course we took their gold, then came back the next year and
demanded more.

"We could see they were weak, and we decided to seize their
lands. One year we didn't go home for the winter, and prepared
for war. Fighters flocked to us, and by the spring we had so
many warriors the Saxons called us The Great Army. Our leaders
were Ragnar Lothbrok's sons, Ivarr and Halfdan. They'd sworn
to avenge him, so we struck Northumbria first. We caught King
Aelle, and made the blood eagle…"

THE VIKING WARS

In the ninth century Scotland, Wales, Ireland and England didn't exist. Ireland was a land of small kingdoms where people spoke Gaelic. The Irish had also settled in the Hebrides and western Scotland. Eastern Scotland belonged to the Picts, a mysterious people with their own language. The original, pre-Roman Britons – the Welsh – had their own ancient tongue, and lived in several kingdoms in the west of Britain.

The Angles and Saxons arrived after the Romans left in the early fifth century. By the end of the sixth century they had conquered eastern and southern Britain, taking over from the Britons. Over the next two centuries they founded kingdoms, gave up their old religion and became Christians, fought each other, and prospered. Then the Vikings came. This time they were led by **Ivarr** and **Halfdan Ragnarsson**, the sons of **Ragnar Lothbrok**. In the 860s **Ivarr** (whose nickname was "the boneless" – nobody really knows why) and **Halfdan** defeated **King Aelle of Northumbria** and killed him. They were said to have "made the blood eagle", which meant cutting out someone's lungs while they were still alive and spreading them out like wings. It probably didn't happen, but it

made a very dramatic story – and terrified their enemies.

*From then on Northumbria was a Viking kingdom, with its capital in the Roman city of York, or **Jorvik** as the Vikings called it. The kingdoms of **Mercia** and **East Anglia** fell to the Vikings next, and by the 870s only the kingdom of **Wessex** stood against them. That nearly fell too, and at one point the young king of Wessex was forced to go into hiding from them with his last few warriors in the marshes of Somerset.*

*His name was Alfred the Great, and he saved Wessex, although he had to keep fighting the Vikings for years. Sometimes he won, and sometimes he had to pay them off. Most were Danes, so such a bribe was called "Danish gold" or **Danegeld**. Eventually he made a treaty with them, giving them control of the lands that became known as the **Danelaw**, covering the Midlands, East Anglia and the North.*

*Alfred dreamed of uniting all the Angles and Saxons, but didn't achieve it. The Vikings were still a threat when he died in 899, and his descendants carried on the struggle. His daughter **Athelflaed** played an important role in the wars that followed. But it was her nephew, Alfred's grandson **Athelstan**,*

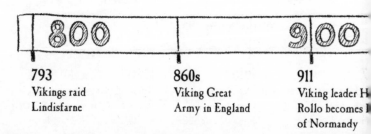

793
Vikings raid
Lindisfarne

860s
Viking Great
Army in England

911
Viking leader H
Rollo becomes I
of Normandy

who finally conquered Viking Northumbria in 927 and became the first king of a new country – England.

Times were changing, though. The Vikings converted to Christianity, and Norway, Sweden and Denmark became more like other countries in Europe. There were fewer Viking raids, but plenty of wars, and several Scandinavian kings became powerful. **Cnut Sweynsson** had a large empire. He became King of England in 1016, King of Denmark in 1018 and King of Norway in 1028 – we remember him as King Canute. The usual date given for the end of the Viking Age is 1066. In the autumn of that year three men fought for the throne of England. The half-Danish, half-Saxon **Harold Godwinson** defeated the great **Harald Hardrada**, King of Norway, at the **Battle of Stamford Bridge** near Jorvik. Then Harold marched south to fight **Duke William of Normandy**, a descendant of Ganger-Hrolf, the Viking who founded Normandy.

They met at the **Battle of Hastings**, and Harold Godwinson lost. Duke William became King of England, and his descendants have been ruling it ever since.

So you could say the Vikings both lost and won.

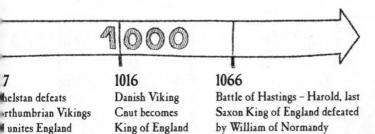

7
helstan defeats
rthumbrian Vikings
unites England

1016
Danish Viking
Cnut becomes
King of England

1066
Battle of Hastings – Harold, last
Saxon King of England defeated
by William of Normandy

The Battle of Hastings, 1066 – the "end" of the Viking Age

"AH, THOSE WERE the days, when a bold Viking could win a kingdom with his sword and a band of brave warriors to stand beside him in the shield-wall! I wish I could return to the land of the living to hear the battle-song of blades once more – although I hear the Christians run things now and it's hard to be a Viking. So I, Skuli, will gladly go back to Valhalla. At least there I'll be able to feast with Odin and talk of old times…"

But as I found out myself, there is no true returning from Valhalla, not until the day of Ragnarok. So I, Gunnar, have sent Skuli back to Odin until that evil day.

And now our journey through the world of the Vikings is nearly over…

And so I bring you home, back to your hall,
wherever that may be. It has been good to journey
with you, but now it is time for us to part.
I have one last gift for you, a poem...

May your dragon-ship ride the waves
And the tomb-dead stay unwoken.
May your sword blade never lose its edge
And your shield-wall be unbroken.

Until we meet again – in this life...
or in Valhalla!

–Your shield-brother, Gunnar Bjornsson

AUTHOR'S NOTE

I was ten when I first encountered the world of the Vikings. My teacher that year was Mr Smith, and I remember liking him, mostly because he read us lots of stories. One was a terrific fantasy adventure, with a hero called Bilbo Baggins, a scary wizard called Gandalf, a crew of dwarfs with funny names – Kili and Fili, Dori, Nori, Ori, Bifur and Bombur – a dragon, a battle…

It was *The Hobbit* by J.R.R. Tolkien, of course, and I thought it was the best story I'd ever heard. I wanted to experience it again, so I joined the library and read it for myself. I borrowed *The Lord of the Rings* and loved that too. How could you not love a story packed with adventure, magic rings, heroes with legendary swords, a gigantic struggle against the forces of darkness that ends in a colossal battle?

I soon discovered that I liked all sorts of stories, but I particularly loved tales of the Vikings. There was something strangely familiar about them and their world. Years later I found out that was because Tolkien had been a professor of Anglo-Saxon and Old Norse at Oxford University, and *The Hobbit* and *The Lord of the Rings* grew out of his love of the Viking myths. That's where he found much of his inspiration, including the names of his dwarfs and Smaug the dragon. Gandalf is also clearly based on

Odin. After all, Gandalf is a sorcerer who wears a wide-brimmed hat, carries a staff, wanders Middle-Earth and fights the forces of darkness. So if you too love the world of the Vikings, I would advise you to seek out Professor Tolkien's books. I would also recommend some modern versions of the Norse myths. My favourites are *Norse Myths; Tales of Odin, Thor and Loki* by Kevin Crossley-Holland, and *Norse Mythology* by Neil Gaiman. Look out too for versions of *The Hávamál* – "The Words of the High One" – on the internet. It's a collection of wise sayings in the form of poems, the High One in question being Odin. It will give you a real insight into the Viking world.

There are some great websites you can look at too. Start with **Jorvik** – https://www.jorvikvikingcentre.co.uk. It's a wonderful place to visit in modern-day York, if you can. I would say the same about the **Viking Ship Museum** near Oslo in Norway – https://www.khm.uio.no/english/visit-us/viking-ship-museum/index.html – and the **Viking Ship Museum in Roskilde**, Denmark – https://www.vikingeskibsmuseet.dk/en/visit-the-museum. They build reconstructions of Viking boats and ships there, and you can book a trip to row like a Viking up the Roskilde Fjord.

A NOTE ON VIKING WORDS IN ENGLISH, AND PLACE-NAMES

The Angles and Saxons spoke an early form of English, the language we speak today. It was quite similar to Norse, so the Angles, Saxons and Vikings could probably understand each other. Lots of Vikings settled in the Danelaw and lived alongside the Angles and Saxons. So it's no surprise the Angles and Saxons picked up many Norse words. We still use them today – in fact they're some of the most common words in English.

Cake (*Caka*)

Call (*Kalla*)

Egg (*Egg*)

Gun (*Gunn, meaning war*)

Keel (*Kjölr*)

Knife (*Knifr*)

Knot (*Knutr*)

Law (*Lögu*)

Mistake (*Mistaka*)

Muck (*Myki, meaning cow dung*)

Outlaw (*Utlagi*)

Skill (*Skil*)

Skip (*Skip*)

Skirt (*Skyrta*)

Skull (*Skulle*)

Sky (*Sky*)

Snub (*Snubba, meaning to curse*)

Thrall, as in "enthralled" (*Thrællæ*)

Ugly (*Uggligr*)

Weak (*Veikr*)

Window (*Vindaugi, meaning "wind-eye"*)

Wrong (*Rangr*)

The Vikings also left their mark in the names of places, especially in Scotland and the north and east of England. The words to look out for are Ness (headland), as in Skegness; Thorpe (a settlement), as in Scunthorpe; By (a settlement or village) as in Whitby. "Gata" in Norse meant street, so in York Coppergate wasn't a gate, but rather the street of the cup makers (Koppari). Mountains in the Lake District are called "Fells", from the Norse word "Fjall", and "Dale" comes from "Dalr" (valley).

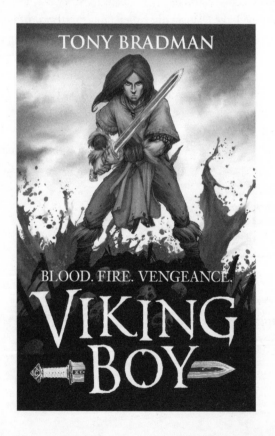

PRAISE FOR VIKING BOY:

"An engaging adventure ... an entertaining and appealing story in its own right."
Booktrust

"Greatly reminiscent of the estimable Rosemary Sutcliff and Geoffrey Trease. Wickedly illustrated throughout (with a few very powerful double page spreads), it's a gorgeous modern spin on the historical novel tradition, all packaged up with Bradman's pacey, accessible prose and some substantial myth and magic."
Did You Ever Stop to Think and Forget to Start Again?

"Whether you are a child or an adult, if you enjoy a thrilling adventure you'll enjoy this book." **TOSTE, TOSTE**

"Packed with action, this exciting story is a fascinating insight into the world of the Vikings." **The Week Junior**

"Couched in excellent research on the period and brings the Viking world to life in a vivid and dramatic way."
fivebooks.com/best-books/viking-history-for-kids/

"Enthralling stuff"
Book for Keeps

Read the story of my journey through the brutal Viking world, to avenge the murder of my father.

PRAISE FOR ANGLO-SAXON BOY:

"In pacey prose for 8-10s, Tony Bradman's *Anglo-Saxon Boy* lays out the adventures that befall Magnus, son of Harold Godwinson, in the run-up to the Battle of Hastings. It is underpinned by historical fact (Magnus existed), and includes, satisfyingly, a grandmother who leads troops, as the story chronicles the making of a warrior." **The Sunday Times**

"The action is fast-paced and the historic detail accurate. The reader is swept along with Magnus as his quest continues. Most know what happened to Harold, but this book explores why. The ending does not disappoint." **The Historical Novel Society**

Winner of the
YOUNG QUILLS HISTORICAL FICTION AWARD

Follow me on my dangerous Anglo-Saxon journey to the Battle of Hastings.

TONY BRADMAN is an award-winning author, editor and reviewer of children's books. He has written poetry, picture books and stories for all ages, including historical fiction set in a wide range of periods, from Roman Britain to the First and Second World Wars. For Walker he has written the bestselling *Viking Boy*, a gripping, immersive adventure story that has become a standard text for children learning about the Vikings; and the award-winning *Anglo-Saxon Boy*, which explores the Battle of Hastings through the eyes of Magnus, son of Harold, the last Saxon king. Tony is also the editor behind the highly successful Voices series of novels by writers such as Benjamin Zephaniah and Patrice Lawrence, about the hidden diverse communities of Britain's history.

About *Viking Boy: The Real Story*, Tony says: "I've loved everything about the Vikings since I was a boy and discovered stories by great writers such as Rosemary Sutcliff and Henry Treece. My novel *Viking Boy* grew out of a desire to write a story that I would have loved to read when I was young. So I was delighted when Walker suggested I write a non-fiction book for children about the Vikings, to be a companion and shield-brother to that book. I loved every second of the research that went into *Viking Boy: The Real Story*, and the writing too. It was a joy to breathe life into the characters of *Viking Boy* once more, so they can tell readers about themselves and their world."